THOMAS ANDREWS
SHIPBUILDER

Reprint from the 1912 original

Additional Foreword by Thorsten Totzke

Impressum
Text: Shan F. Bullock
Foreword: Thorsten Totzke
Pictures Foreword: Thorsten Totzke Collection
Cover: © Copyright Thorsten Totzke

Publisher: Peter Brumm
Dankerskamp 20
22419 Hamburg

THOMAS ANDREWS
SHIPBUILDER

Foreword by Thorsten Totzke

Thomas Andrews Shipbuilder

Foreword

During my over 35 years collecting and researching on Titanic I have met many people who share this hobby with me.

In Titanic circles it is common practice for every detail about the ship and her people to be discussed in detail, (and on occasion, even argued about).

Such a legend was the man known as Thomas Andrews and such a large shadow has his legacy and reoutation cast that in all my years of research into the doomed ship I have never heard a single bad word uttered about the man.

Thomas Andrews jr.

Thomas Andrews Jr. was the son of Thomas Andrews Sen. and his wife Eliza Pirrie. Eliza was the sister of William Pirrie, the managing director of Harland & Wolff shipyard.

In 1889 a young Thomas Andrews began a career at the Harland and Wolff shipyard in Belfast. By all accounts, he was a brilliant and dedicated employee and his rise up the ranks of the company came rapidly. As early as 1901 he was the head of the design department and in 1907 he was the technical director of the shipyard. Together with Alexander Carlisle, he is considered one of the chief designers of the Olympic and Titanic.

Alexander Carlisle

On 24 June 1908 Andrews married Helen Reilly Barbour, the daughter of John Barbour, one of the directors of Harland & Wolff. On 27 November 1910 the couple's only child, Elizabeth Law Barbour Andrews, was born, named Elba.

Due to his respected position, Thomas Andrews headed the shipyard guarantee group on the maiden voyage of the Titanic and left Belfast with her on 2 April 1912.

Thomas Andrew jr. Memorial Hall, Comber

At the time of the collision with the iceberg, Andrews was in his cabin. Afterwards, together with Captain Smith, he assessed the damage to the ship and predicted that she would likely sink within a few short hours.
According to survivors, Andrews assisted with the evacuation of Titanic's passengers and did his very best to ensure that calm and order reigned on the decks of the ill fated liner. He was last seen in the first-class smoking room just before the ship took her final plunge to the bottom.
Thomas Andrews went down with Titanic. His body was never found.
Following the death of Thomas Andrews on Titanic, his widow married Henry Peirson Harland in 1917. (Henry was a member of the Harland

family who were one of the original founders of Harland & Wolff). The couple had four children. Helen eventually passed away in Northern Ireland on 22 August 1966.

The daughter of Thomas Andrews and Helen Barbour, Elizabeth Andrews, remained unmarried. She became a safari guide in Kenya, served as a Red Cross nurse during World War II, and died in a car accident in Ireland in 1973.

In the home town of Thomas Andrews, Comber, one of the earliest and most substantial memorials for a single victim of the Titanic disaster was built in the form of a gathering hall. The Thomas Andrews Jr. Memorial Hall was opened in January 1914.

The architects were Young and McKenzie with sculpted work being commissioned by the artist Sophia Rosamond Praeger. The hall is now maintained by the South Eastern Education Board and used by The Andrews Memorial Primary School. An Ulster History Circle blue plaque is located on his house in Windsor Avenue, Belfast.

Today, the White Sta Line tender, SS Nomadic, is the sole surviving ship designed by Thomas Andrews and yet his legacy of kindness and courage carry on to modern times. In 2004, the asteroid 245158 was named in his honour.

The original biography, Thomas Andrews: Shipbuilder was published shortly after his death. Original first editions of the work are considered sought after collector's items today.

Thorsten Totzke

THOMAS ANDREWS SHIPBUILDER

By Shan F. Bullock

With an Introduction by Sir Horace Plunkett

"... Summoned to the deep,
Thou, thou and all thy mates, to keep
An incommunicable sleep.—WORDSWORTH.

MAUNSEL & COMPANY, LTD.
DUBLIN AND LONDON
1912

First Edition .... October, 1912.
Second Edition .... October, 1912.

This Edition .... May 2020

TO THE MEN WITH WHOM
THOMAS ANDREWS WORKED
WHO KNEW AND LOVED HIM
I DEDICATE THIS BRIEF
STORY OF HIS LIFE

Thomas Andrews Shipbuilder

LIST OF ILLUSTRATIONS

Portrait of Thomas Andrews
(Photo by Abernethy)

Ardara, Comber
(Photo by R. Welch)

HARLAND & WOLFF'S TURBINE ERECTING SHOP
(Photo by R. Welch)

THE TURNING SHOP
(Photo by R. Welch)

THE " TITANIC " AND " OLYMPIC " BUILDING IN THE LARGEST GANTRY IN THE WORLD
(Photo by R. Welch)

THE "TITANIC" LEAVING BELFAST
(Photo by R. Welch)

Thomas Andrews Shipbuilder

INTRODUCTION

Mr. SHAN BULLOCK, who needs no introduction to those who read Irish books, has done no better work than in this tribute to one of the noblest Irishmen Ulster has produced in modern times. I refer not only to the literary merits of Thomas Andrews, Shipbuilder, which speak for themselves, but rather to the true insight with which he has fulfilled the precise purpose held in view by those who asked him to write this little memorial volume. What that purpose was must be known in order that the story itself, and the manner of the telling, may be fully appreciated.

The book was written at the request of a few Irishmen, myself among them, who work together in a movement which seeks to develop agriculture, and generally to improve the condition of our rural communities. We are deeply interested in the great achievements of Ulster industry, because we hold strongly that the prosperity of our country depends largely upon the mutual understanding and the coordination of effort between the two great economic interests into which the Irish, in common with most civilised peoples, are divided.

For this consummation Ireland needs, in our opinion, industrial leaders with a broader conception of the life of the country as a whole. For such leaders we naturally look, more especially those of us whose eyes are turning towards the westering sun, to the younger men. Among these none seemed to us so ideally fitted to give practical expression to our hopes as Thomas Andrews. Thus it was the sense of the great loss the country had sustained which set us thinking how the life of the shipbuilder who had died so nobly could be given its due place in the history of our times—how the lesson of that life could be handed down to the builders of ships and of other things in the Ireland of our dreams.

The project having so originated, the proper treatment of the subject had to be determined. Unquestionably Thomas Andrews was a hero. The wise Bishop Berkeley has said : " Every man, by consulting his own heart, may easily know whether he is or is not a patriot, but it is not easy for the bystander." A man cannot thus know whether he is or is not a hero. Both he and the bystander must wait for the occasion to arise, and the opportunities for exhibiting heroism are as rare and perilous as those for exhibiting patriotism are common and safe.

To Thomas Andrews the supreme test came—came in circumstances demanding almost superhuman fortitude and self-control. Here was not the wild excitement of battle to sustain him; death had to be faced calmly in order that others—to whom he must not even bid farewell—might live. And so in his last hour we see this brave, strong, capable and lovable man displaying, not only heroism, but every quality which had exalted him in the regard of his fellows and endeared him to all who had worked and lived with him. This is the verdict of his countrymen now that the facts of that terrible disaster are fully known.

Yet it was far from our purpose to have the tragedy of the Titanic written with Thomas Andrews as the hero. We deemed it better to place the bare facts before some writer of repute, not one of his personal friends, and ask him to tell in simple language the plain tale of his life so far as it could be gleaned from printed and written records, from his family, friends, and employers; above all, from those fellow-workers—his "pals" as he liked to call them—to whom this book is most fittingly dedicated. The story thus pieced together would be chiefly concerned with his work, for his work was his life.

To Thomas Andrews the hero, then, we did not propose to raise a monument. To his memory a fine memorial hall is to be built and endowed in his native Comber by the inhabitants of the town and district and his friends, while he will be associated in memorials elsewhere with those who died nobly in the wreck. *

These tributes will serve to remind us how he died, but will not tell us how he lived. It is the purpose of this short memoir to give a fairly complete record of his life—his parentage, his home, his education, his pleasures, his tastes and his thoughts, so far as they are known, upon things which count in the lives of peoples. The family, and all from whom information was sought, responded most cordially to our wishes. There remained the difficulty of finding a writer who could tell the story of Thomas Andrews the man, as we wished it to be told.

For such a task it was decided that, if he could be induced to undertake it, the right man was Shan Bullock. He is an Ulsterman, a writer of tales of Ulster life, distinguished among other Irish books by their sincerity and unequalled understanding of the Ulster character. While other Irish writers of imagination and genius have used Irish life to express their own temperament, Shan Bullock has devoted his great literary ability almost entirely to the patient, living and sincere study of what Ulster really is in itself as a community of men and women. It is true that his stories are of rural and agricultural communities, while the scene is now laid chiefly in a great centre of manufacturing industry. But in Mr. Bullock's studies it is always the human factor that predominates. One feels while reading one of his tales that he loves to look upon a man, especially an Ulster man. Here was the ideal historian of the life of Thomas Andrews.

---

* In Belfast a memorial to Thomas Andrews and the other Belfast men who died in the wreck has been generously sub-scribed to by the citizens, and by the Queen's Island workers. He is also included amongst those to whom a similar memorial is to be erected in Southampton. The Reform Club in Belfast is honouring his memory

WITH A TABLET.

It fell to me to approach Mr. Bullock. I induced him to go and see the family, having arranged with them to bring him into touch with the authorities at the Island Works, who were to show him round and introduce him to many who knew our friend.

He promised me that he would look over all the material out of which the story could be pieced to-gether, and that if he found that it "gripped" him and became a labour of love he would undertake it. The story did, as the reader will see, grip him, and grip him hard, and in telling it Mr. Bullock has rendered the greatest of all his services to lovers of truth told about Ireland by Irish writers.

It will now, I think, be clear why Thomas Andrews has, notwithstanding his noble end, been represented as the plain, hard-working Ulster boy, growing into the exemplary and finally the heroic Ulster man that we knew. We see him ever doing what his hand found to do, and doing it with his might. Our author, rightly as I think, makes no attempt to present him as a public man; for this captain of industry in the making was wholly absorbed in his duties to the great Firm he served.

None the less I am convinced that the public side of the man would not long have remained un-developed—who knows but that this very year would have called him forth?—because he had to my personal knowledge the right public spirit. Concentration upon the work in hand prevented his active participation in public affairs, but his mastery over complicated mechanical problems—his power to use materials—and to organise bodies of men in their use, would not, I believe, have failed him if he had come to deal with the mechanics of the nation.

These may be fruitless speculations now, and Mr. Bullock wisely leaves us to draw our own conclusions as to the eminence to which Thomas

Andrews might have attained had his life been spared. Abundant proof of the immense influence he might have exercised is furnished in the eloquently sincere grief which pervades the letters of condolence that poured into the home of the parents at Comber when it was known that they had lost their distinguished son.

They came — over seven hundred of them—from all sorts and conditions of men, ranging from a duke to a pauper in a workhouse.

In one of these letters, too intimate to publish, a near relative pays to the dead shipbuilder a pathetically simple tribute with which I may well leave to the reader Mr Bullock's tale of a noble life and heroic death. "There is not," ran this fine epitaph, "a better boy in heaven."

HORACE PLUNKETT.

Thomas Andrews Shipbuilder

THOMAS ANDREWS
SHIPBUILDER

I.

FOR six generations the Andrews family has been prominent in the life of Comber: that historic and prospering village, near Strangford Lough, on the road from Belfast to Downpatrick: and in almost every generation some one or other of the family has attained distinction.

During the eventful times of 1779-82, John Andrews raised and commanded a company of Volunteers, in which his youngest son, James, served as Lieutenant. Later, another John Andrews was High Sheriff of Down in 1857; and he also it was who founded the firm of John Andrews & Co., which to-day gives employment to some six hundred of the villagers. The present head of the family, William Drennan Andrews, LL.D., was a Judge of the High Court, Ireland, from 1882, and has been a Privy Councillor since 1897. His brother, Thomas Andrews, is a man whose outstanding merits and sterling character have won him an honoured place among Ulstermen.

One of the famous Recess Committee of 1895, he is President of the Ulster Liberal Unionist Association, Chairman of the Belfast and County Down Railway Company, a Privy Councillor, a Deputy Lieutenant of Down, High Sheriff of the same county, and Chairman of its County Council. Two more brothers, James and John, were Justices of the Peace.

In 1870 Thomas Andrews married Eliza Pirrie, a descendant of the Scotch Hamiltons, Lord Pirrie's sister, and herself a woman of the noblest type.

To these, and of such excellent stock, was born, on February 7th, 1873, a son, named after his father, and described in the family record as Thomas Andrews of Dunallan.

His eldest brother, John Miller, born in 1871, and his youngest brother, William, born in 1886, are now Managing Directors of John Andrews & Co., Ltd., under the Chairmanship of their father. A third brother, James, born in 1877, adopted the profession of his distinguished uncle, and is now a barrister-at-law. His only sister, Eliza Montgomery, married in 1906, Lawrence Arthur, the third son of Jesse Hind, Esq., J.P., of Edwalton, Notts, and a solicitor of the Supreme Court.

Tom was, we are told, "a healthy, energetic, bonny child, and grew into a handsome, plucky and lovable boy." His home training was of the wisest, and of a kind, one thinks, not commonly given to Ulster boys in those more austere times of his youth. "No one," writes his brother John, "knew better than Tom how much he owed to that healthy home life in which we were brought up.

We were never otherwise treated than with more than kindness and devotion, and we learned the difference between right and wrong rather by example than by precept." To Tom, his father, then and always, was as an elder brother, full of understanding and sympathy; nor did his mother, even to the end, seem to him other than a sister whose life was as his own. He and his elder brother, John, were inseparable comrades, there among the fields of Comber and in their beautiful home, with its old lawn and gardens, its avenue winding past banks of rhododendrons, the farm behind, outside the great mill humming busily, and in front the gleam of Strangford Lough.

Both father and mother being advocates of temperance, encouraged their lads to abstain from tobacco and strong drink; and to this end their good

ARDARA, COMBER

mother offered to give a tempting prize to such of her sons as could on their twenty-first birthday say they had so abstained.

Tom, and each of his brothers, not only claimed his prize but continued throughout life to act upon the principles it signalised. Doubtless at times, being human boys, they fell into mischief: but only once, their father states, was bodily punishment given to either, and then, as fate willed it, he boxed the ear of the wrong boy!

Quite early, young Tom, like many another lad, developed a fondness for boats, and because of his manifest skill in the making of these he gained among his friends the nickname of „Admiral." In other respects also the man who was to be showed himself in the boy. He had a beautiful way with children. He loved animals of every kind and had over them such influence that they would follow him and come to his call. Still at Ardara, in shelter of the hedge, you may see his nine hives of bees, among which he used to spend many happy hours, and to which in later times he devoted much of his hard-won leisure: once, his mother will tell you, spending a whole winter's day— and a hunting day too !—carrying his halffamished workers to and fro between hive and kitchen in his cap.

For horses he had a passion, and particularly for the Shetland pony given to him one birthday. The fiercest brute yielded to his quiet mastery; he never used whip or spur; and in time he was known as one of the straightest and most fearless riders to hounds in County Down.

Until the age of eleven he was educated privately by a tutor, but in September, 1884, he became a student at the Royal Academical Institution, Belfast—the same institution through which, some years previously, his father and his uncle, then Mr. Pirrie, had passed.

There he showed no special aptitudes, being fonder apparently of games than of study, and not yet having developed those powers of industry for which, soon, he became notable. In the Institution, however, was no more popular boy, both with masters and schoolfellows. He excelled at cricket, one is glad to know, and at all manly sports.

Even then, we are told, generosity and a fine sympathy were prominent traits in his character. "He was always happy," writes a playmate, "even-tempered, and showed a developing power of impressing everyone with his honesty and simplicity of purpose."

Wherever he went Tom carried his own sunshine. All were fond of him. One can see him returning with his brother from school, big, strong, well-favored, and perhaps with some premonition of what the future had in store, lingering sometimes near the station doorway to watch the great ships rising above the Island Yard close by and to listen for a minute to the hammers beating some great vessel into shape: and whilst he stands there, grave and thought-ful for a minute, one may write here the judg-ment of his parents upon him, "He never caused us a moment's anxiety in his life."

II.

WHEN he was sixteen, on the ist May, 1889, Tom left school, and as a premium apprentice entered the shipyard of Messrs. Harland & Wolff.

In one important respect the date of his entry may be accounted fortunate, for about that time, chiefly through the enterprise of the White Star Company in the matter of constructing a fleet of giant ships for the Atlantic service, great developments were imminent, if not already begun, in the shipping world. To a boy of sixteen, however, the change from the comforts of home and the comparative freedom of school-life to the stern discipline of the yards must have been exacting.

It was work now, and plenty of it, summer and winter, day in day out, the hardest he could do at the hardest could be given him. He was to be tested to the full. With characteristic wisdom, Mr. Pirrie had decided that no favour whatever was to be shown the boy on the score of relationship. By his own efforts and abilities he must make his way, profiting by no more than the inspiration of his uncle's example: and if he failed, well, that too was a way many another had gone before him.

But Tom was not of the breed that fails. He took to his work instantly and with enthusiasm. Distance from home necessitated his living through the workaday week in Belfast. Every morning he rose at ten minutes to five and was at work in the Yard punctually by six o'clock.

His first three months were spent in the Joiner's shop, the next month with the Cabinet makers, the two following months working in ships. There followed two months in the Main store; then five with the Shipwrights, two in the Moulding loft, two with the Painters, eight with the iron Shipwrights, six with the Fitters, three with the Pattern-makers, eight with the Smiths. A long spell of eighteen months in the Drawing office completed his term of five years as an apprentice.

Throughout that long ordeal Tom inspired everyone who saw him, workmen, foremen, managers, and those in higher authority, as much by the force of his personal character as by his qualities of industry. Without doubt here was one destined to success. He was thorough to the smallest detail. He mastered everything with the ease of one in love with his task.

We have a picture of him drawn by a comrade, in his moleskin trousers and linen jacket, and instinctively regarded by his fellow-apprentices as their leader, friend and adviser in all matters of shipyard lore and tradition. "He was some steps ahead of me in his progress through the Yard," the account goes on, "so I saw him only at the breakfast and luncheon hours, but I can remember how encouraging his cheery optimism and unfailing friendship were to one who found the path at times far from easy and the demands on one's patience almost more than could be endured."

Many a workman, too, with whom he wrought at that time will tell you today, and with a regret at his untimely loss as pathetic as it is sincere, how faithful he was, how upstanding, generous. He would work at full pressure in order to gain time to assist an old workman "in pulling up his job." He would share his lunch with a mate, toil half the night in relief of a fellow-apprentice who had been overcome by sickness, or would plunge gallantly into a flooded hold to stop a leakage.

"It seemed his delight," writes a foreman, "to make those around him happy. His was ever the friendly greeting and the warm handshake and kind disposition." Such testimony is worth pages of outside eulogy, and testimony of its kind, from all sorts and conditions, exists in abundance.

The long day's work over at the Island, many a young man would have preferred, and naturally perhaps, to spend his evenings pleasurably: not so

Tom Andrews. Knowing the necessity, if real success were to be attained, of perfecting himself on the technical as much as on the practical side of his profession, and perhaps having a desire also to make good what he considered wasted opportunities at school, he pursued, during the five years of his apprenticeship, and afterwards too, a rigid course of night studies: in this way gaining an excellent knowledge of Machine and Freehand drawing, of Applied mechanics, and the theory of Naval architecture.

So assiduously did he study that seldom was he in bed before eleven o'clock; he read no novels, wasted no time over newspapers; and hardly could be persuaded by his friends to give them his company for an occasional evening. His weekly game of cricket or hockey, with a day's hunting now and then or an afternoon's yachting on the Lough, gave him all the relaxation he could permit himself; and by 1894, when his term of apprenticeship ended, the thrill of bitting a ball over the boundary (and Tom was a mighty hitter who felt the thrill often) was experienced with less and still less frequency, whilst sometimes now, and more frequently as time went on, the joy of spending Sunday with his dear folk at Comber had to be foregone.

Even when the Presidency of the Northern Cricket Union was pressed upon him, such were the stern claims of duty that the pleasure of accepting it had ruthlessly to be sacrificed.

What grit, what zest and sense of duty, the boy—for he was no more—must have had, so to labour and yet to thrive gloriously ! Perfect health, his sound physique, his sunny nature, and strict adherence to the principles of temperance encouraged by his mother, helped him to attain fine manhood. During the period of bis apprenticeship he was up to time on every morning of the five years except one—and of his doings on that fateful morning a story is told which, better perhaps than any other, throws light upon his character.

HARLAND AND WOLFF'S TURBINE ERECTING SHOP

It was a good custom of the firm to award a gold watch to every pupil who ended his term without being late once. That morning Tom's clock had failed to ring its alarm at the usual time, so despite every endeavour the boy could not reach the gates before ten minutes past six. He might, by losing the whole day and making some excuse, have escaped penalty: instead, he waited outside the gates until eight o'clock and went in to work at the breakfast hour.

One other story relating to this period is told by his mother. It too reveals distinctive points of character.

On an occasion Tom, with several fellow- pupils, went on a walking tour during the Easter holidays over the Ards peninsula. Crossing Strangford Lough at Portaferry, they visited St. John's Point, the most easterly part of Ireland; then, finding the tide favourable, crossed the sands from Baliykinler to Dundrum— Tom carrying the youngest of the party on his back through a deep intervening stretch of water—and thence, by way of Newcastle, proceeded across the mountains to Rostrevor.

In their hotel at Rostrevor the boys, during an excess of high spirits, broke the rail of a bedstead; whereupon Tom, assuming responsi-bility, told the landlady that he would bear the expense of repairing the break. She answered that in her hotel they did not keep patched beds, consequently would be troubling him for the cost of a new one.

"If so, the old one belongs to me," said Tom.
"Provided you'll be taking it away," countered the dame.

The boy argued no further, but finding presently, through a friendly chambermaid, an old charwoman who said her sick husband would rejoice in the luxury of the bedstead, he offered to mend it and give it to her.

"Ah, but wouldn't it be more than my place is worth, child dear," she answered, "for the like of me to be taking it from the hotel."

"Never mind that," said Tom. "Give me your address, borrow a screw driver, and I'll see to it."

So he and his companions, having roughly repaired the rail, took the bedstead to pieces, and, applauded by the visitors, carried it to the street. A good-natured tram conductor allowed them to load their burden on an end of his car.

Soon they reached the woman's home, bore in the bedstead, set it up in the humble room, raised the old man and his straw mattress upon it from the floor, made him comfortable, and dowered with all the blessings the old couple could invoke upon them, went away happy.

III.

So much impressed was the firm with Tom's industry and capacity that, soon after the time of his entering the Drawing Office in November, 1892, he was entrusted with the discharge of responsible duties. It is on record that in February, 1893, he was given the supervision of construction work on the Mystic; that in November of the same year he represented the firm, to its entire satisfaction and his own credit, on the trials of the White Star Liner Gothic; whilst, immediately following the end of his apprenticeship in May, 1894, he helped the Shipyard Manager to examine the Coptic, went to Liverpool and reported on the damage done to the Lycia, and in November discussed with the General Manager and Shipyard Manager the Notes in connection with the renovation of the Germanic—that famous Liner, still capable after twenty-five years on the Atlantic Service of making record passages, but now crippled through being overladen with ice at New York.

In 1894 he was twenty-one years old: a man and well launched on his great career.

It is not necessary, and scarcely possible, to follow Andrews with any closeness as rapidly, step by step, he climbed the ladder already scaled, with such amazing success, by Mr. Pirrie. The record of his career is written in the wonderful story of the Queen's Island Yard through all its developments onward from 1894, and in the story of the many famous ships repaired and built during the period.

The remarkable engineering feat of lengthening the Scot and the Augusta Victoria, by dividing the vessels and inserting a section amidships; the reconstruction of the China after its disaster at Perim and of the Paris following its wreck on the Manacles: in these operations, covering roughly the years 1896 – 1900, Andrews, first as an outside Manager and subsequently as Head of the Repair department, took a distinguished part. He was growing, widening knowledge, maturing capacity, and both by the Staff, and by those in touch with the Yard, he became recognised as what the watching crowd terms, not unhappily, a coming man.

Having made his mark in the Repair Department, Andrews was next to prove himself on construction work.

Prior to the launch of the Oceanic in 1899, and whilst engaged in the reconstruction operations already mentioned, he had also rendered good service at the building of ships for many of the great steamship lines; but it was perhaps with the building of the Celtic (1899-1901), when he became Manager of Construction Work, that the path of his career took him swiftly up into prominence.

The duty of supervising all the structural details of the vessel brought him into close practical touch with the Drawing office, the Moulding loft, the Platers' shops, and all the other Departments through which he had passed as an apprentice; imposed upon his young shoulders great responsibilities tested his capacity for handling men; put him in constant and intimate view of his employers; widened his relations with owners, contractors, directors, managers; opened to him not only the life of the Yard, but the vast outer life of the Shipping and Commercial world, and in a hundred other respects helped towards his development as a shipbuilder and a man.

Now he had opportunity to apply his knowledge and experience, to express in tangible torm his genius. The great ship rising there below the gantries to the accompaniment of such clang and turmoil—she was his, part of him.

To the task, one of the noblest surely done by men, he gave himself unsparingly, every bit of him, might and main: and his success, great as it was, had the greater acclaim because in achieving it he worked not for personal success but for success in his work. That was the man's way. His job, first and last and always.

The names alone of all the ships in whose building Andrews had a hand, more or less, as Designer, Constructor, Supervisor and Adviser, would fill this page. The Cedric, the Baltic, the Adriatic, the Oceanic, the Amerika, the President Lincoln and President Grant, the Nieuw Amsterdam, the Rotterdam, the Lapland (of which recently we have heard so much): those are a few of them.

The Olympic and the Titanic: those are two more. Their names are as familiar to us as those of our friends. We have, some of us, seen the great ships on whose bows they are inscribed, perhaps sailed in them, or watched anxiously for their arrival at some port of the world; well, wherever they sail now, or lie, they have upon them the impress of Tom Andrews' hand and brain, and with one of them, the last and finest of all, he himself gloriously perished.

There are many others, less known perhaps, but carrying the flag no less proudly upon the Seven seas, for whose design and construction
Andrews was in some measure, often in great measure responsible: the Aragon, the Amazon, the Avon, the Asturias, the Arlanza, the Herefordshire, the Leicestershire, the Gloucestershire, the Oxfordshire, the Pericles, the Themistocles, the Demosthenes, the Laurentic, the Megantic, and the rest. It is a splendid record. Lord Pirrie may well be proud of it, and Ulster too : both we know are proud of the man who so devotedly helped to make it.

The work of building all those ships, and so many more, from the Celtic to the Titanic, covered a period of some thirteen years, 1899- 1912, and in that period Andrews gained such advancement as his services to the Firm deserved. In 1904 he became Assistant Chief Designer, and in the year following was promoted to be Head of the Designing department under Lord Pirrie. His age then was thirty-two, an age at which most men are beginning their career; but he already had behind him what may seem the work and experience of a strenuous lifetime.

"When first I knew Mr. Andrews," writes one who knew him intimately, and later was closely associated with him in his work, "he was a young man, but young as he was to him were entrusted the most important and responsible duties—the direct supervision of constructing the largest ships built in the Yard from the laying of their keels until their sailing from Belfast.

Such a training eminently fitted him for the important position to which he succeeded in 1905, that of Chief of the Designing department. For one so young the position involved duties that taxed him to the full. To superintend the construction of ships like the Baltic and Oceanic was a great achievement, but at the age of thirty-two to be Chief of a department designing leviathans like the Olympic was a greater one still. How well he rose to the call everyone knows.

No task was too heavy, and none too light, for him to grapple with successfully. He seemed endowed with boundless energy, and his interest in his work was unceasing."

Others who knew him well during this important period of his career testify in the like manner.

"Diligent to the point of strenuousness," wrote one of them, "thinking whilst others slept, reading while others played, through sheer toil and ability he made for himself a position that few of his years attain"; and then the writer, whose ideal of life is character, notes approvingly and justly that Andrews worked not as a hireling, but in the spirit of an artist whose work must satisfy his own exacting conscience.

Those boundless energies soon were given wider scope. Early in 1907 the Adriatic was finished, and in March of that same year he was made a Managing Director of the Firm, the Right Hon. A. M. Carlisle being at this time Chairman of the Board. Everyone knows, or can judge for himself, what were the duties of this new position—this additional position, rather, for he still remained Chief of the Designing department—and what, in such a huge and complicated concern as the Island works, the duties involved. Briefly we may summarise them.

A knowledge of its fifty-three branches equal to that of any of the fifty-three men in charge of them; the supervising these, combining and managing them so that all might, smoothly and efficiently, work to the one great end assigned, the keeping abreast with the latest devices in labour-saving appliances, with the newest means of securing economical fitness, with the most modern discoveries in electrical, mechanical and marine engineering—in short, everything relative to the construction and equipment of modern steamships; and in addition all the numerous and delicate duties devolving upon him as Lord Pirrie's Assistant.

Furthermore, the many voyages of discovery, so to speak, which he made as representative of the Firm, thereby, we are told by one with whom he sailed often, "gaining a knowledge of sea life and the art of working a ship unequalled in my experience by anyone not by profession a seafarer"; and, lastly, his many inspections of, and elaborate reports upon, ships and business works, together with his survey, at Lord Pirrie's instance, of the Harbours of Ireland, Canada, Germany, and elsewhere.

It seems a giant's task. Even to us poor humdrum mortals, toiling meanly on office stools at our twopenny enterprises, it seems more than a giant's task. Yet Andrews shouldered it, unweariedly, cheerily, joyfully, for pure love of the task.

One sees him, big and strong, a paint- smeared bowler hat on his crown, grease on his boots and the pockets of his blue jacket stuffed with plans, making his daily round of the Yards, now consulting his Chief, now conferring with a foreman, now interviewing an owner, now poring over intricate calculations in the Drawing office, now in company with his warm friend, old schoolfellow, and co-director, Mr. George Gumming of the Engineering department, superintending the hoisting of a boiler by the two hundred ton crane into some newly launched ship by a wharf.

Or he runs amok through a gang—to their admiration, be it said—found heating their teacans before hornblow; or comes unawares upon a party enjoying a stolen smoke below a tunnel-shaft, and, having spoken his mind forcibly, accepts with a smile the dismayed sentinel's excuse that " 'twasn't fair to catch him by coming like that into the tunnel instead of by the way he was expected." Or he kicks a red hot rivet, which has fallen fifty feet from an upper deck, missing his head by inches, and strides on laughing at his escape. Or he calls some laggard to stern account, promising him the gate double quick without any talk next time. Or he lends a ready hand to one in difficulties; or just in time saves another from falling down a hold; or saying that married men's lives are precious, orders back a third from some dangerous place and himself takes the risk. Or he runs into the Drawing office with a hospital note and a gift of flowers and fruit for the sick wife of a draughtsman. Or at horn-blow he stands by a ship's gangway, down which four thousand hungry men, with a ninety feet drop below them, are rushing for home and supper, and with voice and eye controls them ... a guard rope breaks . . . another instant and there may be grim panic on the gangway . . . but his great voice rings out, "Stand back, men," and he holds them as in a leash until the rope is made good again.

All in the day's work, those and a thousand other incidents which men treasure to-day in the Island, and, if you are tactful, will reveal to you in their slow laconic Northern way. He has been in the Yard perhaps since four or five o'clock—since six for a certainty. At seven or so he will trudge home, or ride in a tramcar with the other workers, to sit over his plans or his books well into the night.

One recalls a day, not long ago, spent most of it in tramping over the Island Works, guided by two men who had worked for many years with Andrews and who, like others we saw and thousands we did not see, held his memory almost in reverence. In and out, up and down we went, through heat and rain, over cobble stones and tram lines; now stepping on planks right down the double bottom, three hundred yards long, from which was soon to rise the Titanic's successor; now crouching amongst the shores sustaining the huge bulk of another halfplated giant; now passing in silent wonder along the huge cradles and ways above which another monster stood ready for launching.

Then into shop after shop in endless succession, each needing a day's journey to traverse, each wonderfully clean and ordered, and all full of wonders. Boilers as tall as houses, shafts a boy's height in diameter, enormous propellers hanging like some monstrous sea animal in chains, turbine motors on which workmen clambered as upon a cliff, huge lathes, pneumatic hammers, and quiet slowmoving machines that dealt with cold steel, shearing it, punching it, planing it, as if it had been so much dinner cheese.

Then up into the Moulding Loft, large enough for a football ground, and its floor a beautiful maze of frame lines; on through the Joiners' shops, with their tools that can do everything but speak; through the Smiths' shops, with their long rows of helmet-capped hearths, and on into the great airy building, so full of interest that one could linger in it for a week, where an army of Cabinetmakers are fashioning all kinds of ship's furniture. Then across into the Central power station, daily generating enough electricity to light Belfast. On through the fine arched Drawing hall, where the spirit of Tom Andrews seemed still to linger, and into his office where often he sat drafting those reports, so exhaustively minute, so methodical and neatly penned, which now have such pathetic and revealing interest. Lastly, after such long journeying, out to a wharf and over a great ship, full of stir and clamour, and as thronged with workmen as soon it would be with passengers.

And often, as one went, hour after hour, one kept asking, "Had Mr. Andrews knowledge of this, and this, and that?"
"Yes, of everything—he knew everything," would be the patient answer.
"And could he do this, and this, and this?" one kept on.
"He could do anything," would be the answer.
"Even how to drive an engine?" "Surely."
"And how to rivet a plate?" "He could have built a ship himself, and fitted her—yes, and sailed her too"—was the answer we got; and then as one dragged wearily towards the gateway (outside which, you will remember, young Tom waited one bitter morning, disappointed but staunch) the guide, noting one's plight, said, "You will sleep well to-night?"
Why, yes, one felt like sleeping for a week!
"Ah, well," was the quiet comment, "Mr. Andrews would do all that and more three times maybe every day."

All in the day's work, you see. And when it was done, then home in a tramcar, to have his dinner, a talk with his mother over the telephone, and so to work again until eleven.

In 1901 Andrews became a Member of the Institution of Naval Architects, and in the year following a Member of the Institution of Mechanical Engineers. He was also a Member of the Society of Naval Architects and Marine Engineers (New York), and an Honorary Member of the Belfast Association of Engineers.

In 1908 he made a home for himself at Dunallan, Windsor Avenue, Belfast, marrying, on June 24th, Helen Reilly, younger daughter of the late John Doherty Barbour, of Conway, Dunmurry, County Antrim, D.L.—worthiest and most loyal of helpmates.

Concerning his married life, so woefully restricted in point of years as it was rich in bounty of happiness, it is perhaps sufficient to say here that, just before he sailed from Southampton, in April last, on that final tragic voyage, he made occasion, one evening whilst talking with a friend, to contrast his own lot with the lot of some husbands he knew; saying, amongst other things, that in the whole time since his marriage, no matter how often he had been away or how late he had stayed at the Yard, never had Mrs. Andrews made a complaint.

She would not. With Jane Eyre she could say, "I am my husband's life as fully as he is mine."

In 1910 a child was born to them and named Elizabeth Law Barbour.

IV.

ALL this is important, vital a great deal of it; but after all what concerns us chiefly, in this brief record, is the kind of man Thomas Andrews was—that and the fine end he made. Everything, one supposes, in this workaday world, must eventually be expressed in terms of character. Though a man build the Atlantic fleet, himself with superhuman vigour of hand and brain, and have not character, what profiteth it him, and how much the less profiteth it the fleets maybe, at last?

Perhaps of all the manual professions that of shipbuilding is the one demanding from those engaged in it, masters and men, the sternest rectitude. Good enough in the shipyard is never enough. Think what scamped work, a flawed shaft, a badly laid plate, an error in calculation, may mean some wild night out in the Atlantic ; and when next you are in Belfast go to Queen's Island and see there, in the shops, on the slips, how everyone is striving, or being made to strive, on your behalf and that of all who voyage, for the absolute best—everything to a hair's breadth, all as strong and sound as hands can achieve, each rivet of all the millions in a liner (perhaps the most impressive thing one saw) tested separately and certified with its own chalk mark.

Well, Andrews, to the extent of his powers and position, was responsible for that absolute best, and the fact that he was proves his character—but does not of itself establish his claim to a place high and apart. Many others assuredly have succeeded as speedily and notably as he, taking success at its material valuation, and their names are written, or one day will be written in the sand; but irrespective - of the great work he did and the great success he achieved, Andrews was a man, in the opinion of all who knew him, whose name deserves to be graven in enduring characters: and why that is so has yet, to some extent at least, to be shown.

In appearance he made a fine figure, standing nearly six feet high, weighing some two hundred pounds, well-built, straight, with broad shoulders and great physical development. He had dark brown hair, sharp clean-shaven features; you would call him handsome; his brown eyes met yours with a look of the frankest kindliness, and when he gripped your hand he took you, as it were, to himself.

Even as you see him in a portrait you feel constrained to exclaim, as many did at first sight of him, "Well, thafs a man !" He had a wonderful ringing laugh, an easy way with him, an Irishman's appreciation of humour. He was sunny, big-hearted, full of gaiety. He loved to hear a good story, and could tell yoa one as well as another.

He had the luck to be simple in his habits and pleasures, his food, his dress, his tastes. Give him health, plenty of friends, plenty of work, and occasionally some spare hours in which to enjoy a good book (Maeterlinck's Life of the Bee for preference) and some good music, to go yachting on Strangford Lough, or picnicking at the family bungalow on Braddock Island, or for a long jolly ride with Mrs. Andrews in their little Renault round the Ards Peninsula, and he was thoroughly content. When of a Saturday evening he opened the door, so the servants at Ardara used to say, they like all the rest waiting expectantly for his coming, it was as though a wind from the sea swept into the house. All was astir.

His presence filled the place. Soon you would hear his father's greeting, "Well, my big son, how are you?" and thereafter, for one more week's end, it was in Ardara as though the schoolboy was home for a holiday. You would hear Tom's voice and laugh through the house and his step on the stairs; you would see him, gloved and veiled, out working among his bees, scampering on the lawn with the children, or playing with the dog, or telling many a good story to the family circle.

Everyone loved him—everyone.

A distinguished writer, Mr. Erskine Childers, in an estimate of Andrews, judges that the charm of the man lay in a combination of power and simplicity. Others tell how unassertive he was, and modest in the finest sense; "one of nature's gentlemen," says a foreman who owed him much, no pride at all, ready always to take a suggestion from anyone, always expressing his views quietly and considerately; "having of himself," writes Mrs. Andrews, "the humblest opinion of anyone I ever knew." And then she quotes some lines he liked and wrote in her album :

> "Do what you can, being what you are,
> Shine like a glow-worm, if you cannot as a star,
> Work like a pulley, if you cannot as a crane,
> Be a wheel-greaser, if you cannot drive a train ";

and goes on to say how much Judge Payne's familiar lines express the spirit and motive of his actions throughout life, and how always he had such a love for humanity that everyone with whom he came in contact felt the tremendous influence of his unselfish nature. He was never so happy as when giving and helping.

Many a faltering youth on the threshold of the world he took by the arm and led forward. A shipwright testifies "to his frequent acknowledgment of what others, not so high as himself, tried to do." Another calls him "a kind and considerate chief and a good friend always." A third, in a letter full of heartbreak at his loss, pays him fine tribute: "In the twenty years I have known him I never saw in him a single crooked turn. He was always the same, one of the most even-tempered men I ever worked with." Such spontaneous testimony to character is perhaps sufficient; but one may crown it by repeating a story told, with full appreciation of its value, by his mother.

When King Edward and Queen Alexandra made their memorable visit to Belfast in July, 1903, the line of route passed through the street in which Andrews lived; and to witness the procession he invited to his rooms, all decorated for the occasion and plentifully supplied with dainties, a large party of children. "Well, my dear," one was asked afterwards, "and what did you think of the King?" "The King," answered the child—" oh, cousin Tommy was our King."

Regarding his remarkable powers of application and industry, enough too has perhaps already been written ; but what must be made clear, even at the cost of repetition, for therein lay the man's strength, was the spirit in which he approached the great business of work.

It has been said, and doubtless will be said again, that for one to labour as Andrews did, whatever the incentive or object, is an inhuman process making for narrowness of manhood and a condition of drudgery. Perhaps so. Herbert Spencer once expressed some such opinion. It ia largely a question of one's point of view, to a lesser extent perhaps a matter of aptitude or circumstance. At all events, in this respect, it seems wise to distinguish as between man and man, and work and work; for with the example of Andrews before them even cavillers must admit that what they call drudgery can be well justified.

How he would have laughed had someone, even a Herbert Spencer, called him a drudge ! Anyone less the creature, howevei you regaided him, you could not easily find. Work was his nature, his life; he throve upon it, lived for it, loved it. And think what a work it was! The noblest, one repeats, done by men.

In his dressingroom was hung a framed copy of Henry Van Dyke's well-kriown sonnet. It is worth quoting:

" Let me but do my work from day to day

> In field or forest, at the desk or loom,
> In roaring market-place, or tranquil room;
> Let me but find it in my heart to say,
> When vagrant wishes beckon me astray,
> This is my work, my blessing, not my doom;
> Of all who live, I am the one by whom
> This work can best be done in my own way.
> Then shall I see it not too great nor small,
> To suit my spirit and to prove my powers;
> Then shall I cheerfully greet the labouring hours,
> And cheerful turn, when the long shadows fall
> At eventide, to play, and love, and rest,
> Because I know for me my work is best"

"This is my work, my blessing, not my doom . . . because I know for me my work is best 99: can it be said that the man who worked in the spirit of those words, having them before him like a prayer each morning and each night, was not fulfilling destiny in a noble way?

No mean thought of self, no small striving after worldly success, but always the endeavour to work in his own way to suit bis spirit and to prove his powers. If that way be narrow— well, so is the way narrow that leads to eternal life.

But, it might be said, Andrews had such opportunity and the rare good fortune also to have his spirit suited with work that proved his powers. It was so. Yet one knows certainly that had his opportunity been different he would still have seized it; have been the best engine driver in Ulster or have greased wheels contentedly and with all diligence. One remembers the sentence from Ruskin which he had printed or his Christmas card for 1910: "What we think, or what we know, or wh^t we believe, is in the end of little consequence. The only thing of consequence is what we do."

The best doing, always and every way, one knows how that aspiration would appeal to Andrews, good Unitarian that he was ; just as one knows how Ruskin, he who made roads and had such burning sympathy always with honest workers, would have appreciated Andrews and agreed that the name of such a man should not perish as have the names of most other of the world's great Architects and Builders." Today I commence my twenty-first year at the works, all interesting and happy days.

I would go right back over them again if I could": one feels that the spirit of those words, written by Andrews to his wife on May 1st, 1909, would have appealed to Ruskin; and had he known the man would he not have noted, as did another observer—Professor W. G. S. Adams,* of Oxford—" how it was to the human question the man's mind always turned," and been eager to judge," that here was one who had in him the true stuff of the best kind of captain of industry"?

A captain of industry: the phrase is happy, and convincing too is the passage wherein Mr. Erskine Childers gives his impression of Andrews as, towards the close of 1911, he saw him one day working in the Island Yard.
"It was bracing to be near him," writes Mr. Childers, and then goes on: "His mind seemed to revel in its mastery, both of the details and of the ensemble, both of the technical and the human side of a great science, while restlessly seeking to enlarge its outlook, conquer new problems, and achieve an ever fresh perfection. Whether it was about the pitch of a propeller or the higher problems of design, speed, and mercantile competition, one felt the same grip and enthusiasm and, above all perhaps, the same delight in frank self-revelation."

---

* It is interesting to note the circumstances which brought these two men together. Mr. Adams, who is now Professor of Political Theory and Institutions at Oxford, was then Superintendent of Statistics and Intelligence in the Irish Department of Agriculture and Technical Instruction. He went to Andrews as the man most likely to give him reliable information and sound opinions upon certain industrial questions of interest to the Department. A peculiar value attaches to the high regard in which Thomas Andrews was held by this distinguished political and economic thinker.

V.

WE come back, then, to Andrews as Mr. Childers saw him on that day in the Yard—big, strong, inspiriting, full of enthusiasm and mastery—a genuine captain of industry there on the scene of his triumphs, yet revealing himself as modestly, we know, as any of the great army of workers under his direction.

Before attempting to give some further and completer account of the relations which existed between him and the Islanders, it may be well to give a letter written by Andrews in 1905 to a young relative then beginning work as an engineer :—

"I am sorry I did not get a shake of your fist, old chap, before leaving, just to wish you good luck at your business and a good time at——
"Please accept from me the enclosed small gift to go towards a little pocket-money.

"You are such a sensible boy I know that you require no advice from me, but as an old hand who has come through the mill myself I would just like to say how important it is for you to endeavour to give your employers full confidence in you from the start. This can best be gained:

"(1) By punctuality and close attention to your work at all times—but don't allow your health to suffer through overwork.

"(2) Always carry out instructions given by those above you, whether you agree with them or not—and try to get instructions in writing if you are not sure of your man.

"(3) Always treat those above you with respect, no matter whether they are fools or know less than yourself.

"(4) Never give information unless you are perfectly sure, better to say you are not sure, but will look the matter up.

"(5) Never be anxious to show how quick you are by being the first out of the shop when the horn blows. It is better on these occasions to be a bit slow.

"Now this is a sermon by Thomas, but not one of your father's—only that of an old cousin who has high expectations of you and is interested in your welfare.

"Goodbye and good luck."

That little sermon by Thomas, with its admixture of shrewdness, wisdom, and kind-heartedness, may be taken as embodying the workaday rules of duty perfected by Andrews through a varied experience of sixteen years—rules doubtless as faithfully observed by himself as they were commended for the guidance of others.

What may be called its horse sense, its blunt avowal of how to play the game, helps us towards a fuller understanding of the man, puts him in the plain light through which, every day in view of everyone, he passed. It shows us why he succeeded, why in any circumstances and irrespective almost of his higher qualities, he was bound to succeed. It explains, to some extent, what a workman meant in calling him" a born leader of men."

It helps us to understand why some called him a hard man and why he made a few enemies; helps us also to understand why the Islander who threatened to drop a bag of rivets on his head was treated with laughing amenity. What Andrews demanded of others he exacted in greater measure of himself. If at times he enforced his code of conduct with sternness, in that, as all who felt the weight of his hand would eventually acknowledge, he was but doing his plain duty.

Did men skulk or scamp their job, they must be shown decisively that a shipyard was no place for them. Someone discovered asleep on a nine inch plank spanning an open ventilator must be taught discretion. But no bullying, no unfairness—above all, no show of malice.

If in Andrews' nature was no trace of maliciousness, neither did there lurk in it any meanness. Not once, but a thousand times, during the past black months, has his character been summed with characteristic terseness by the Island shipwrights:
"Just as a judge. . . . Straight as a die. . . . There wasn't a crooked turn in him": simple phrases conveying a magnificent tribute. For what better in anyone can you have than the straightness of a die, whether you regard him as man or master? And such straightness in a shipbuilder is not that the supreme quality?

At all events this quality of absolute rectitude, so indispensable in other respects, was the main quality which, in their personal relations with him, won for Andrews the admiration and esteem of the Islanders. They could trust him.

He would see fair play. "If he caught you doing wrong he wasn't afraid to tell you so." "If he found you breaking a rule he wouldn't fire you straight away, but would give you the rough side of his tongue and a friendly caution." "So long as one reported a mistake honestly he had consideration, but try to hide it away and he blazed at you." "He had a grand eye for good work and a good man, and the man who did good work, no matter who he was, got a clap on the shoulder." So the Islanders, this man and that; and then once more comes the crowning judgment on the tongue of so many," He was straight as a die."

But not that one quality alone gained for Andrews his great, one might say his unique, popularity in the Yard. His vast knowledge, his mastery of detail, his assiduity, his zest: all these merits had their due effect upon the men: and effective too was the desire he showed always to get the best possible out of every worker. It was not enough to do your job, he expected you to think about it: and if from your thinking resulted a suggestion it got his best consideration. It might be worthless— never mind, better luck next time; if it were worth a cent., he would make it shine in your eyes like a dollar.

In addition, were those more personal qualities—emanations, so to speak, of the man's character: his generosity, kindliness, patience, geniality, humour, humility, courage, that great laugh of his, the winning smile, the fine breezy presence: of those also the men had constant and intimate experience.

Anyone in trouble might be sure of his sympathy. After a spell of sickness his handshake and hearty greeting stirred new life in your blood. Once he found a great fellow ill-treating a small foreman who, for sufficient reason, had docked his wages; whereupon Andrews took off his coat and hammered the bully.

During labour and party troubles, he several times, at risk of his life, saved men from the mob. One day, in a gale, he climbed an eighty foot staging, rescued the terrified man who had gone up to secure the loose boards, and himself did the work.

Another day, he lent a hand to a ship¬wright toiling across the yard under

THE TURNING SHOP

a heavy beam, and as they went Andrews asked, "How is it, M'Ilwaine, you always like to be beside me?" "Ah, sir," was the reply, "it is because you carry up well."

These incidents, chosen from so many, enable us to see why, in the words of the Island poet," though Andrews was our master we loved him to a man." He always carried up well," stood four-square to all the winds that blow." Too often, those in authority rule as tyrants, using power like some Juggernaut crushing under the beasts of burden. But Andrews, following the example of his uncle, preferred to rule beneficently as a man among his fellows.

"One evening," writes Mrs. Andrews, "my husband and I were in the vicinity of Queen's Island, and noticing a long file of men going home from work, he turned to me and said, 'There go my pals, Nellie.' I can never forget the tone in his voice as he said that, it was as though the men were as dear to him as his own brothers. Afterwards, on a similar occasion, I reminded him of the words, and he said, 'Yes, and they are real pals too.' "

You see now why a colleague, Mr. Saxon Payne, secretary to Lord Pirrie, could write, "It was not a case of liking him, we all loved him"; and why during those awful days in April, when hope of good news at last had gone, the Yard was shrouded in gloom and rough men cried like women.

They had lost a pal. And not they only. On both sides of the Atlantic, wherever men resort whose business is in the great waters, owners, commanders, directors, managers, architects, engineers, ships officers, stewards, sailors, the name Tom Andrews is honoured to-day as that of one whose remarkable combination of gifts claimed not only their admiration, but their affection.

"What we are to do without Andrews," said a Belfast ship-owner, "I don't know. He was probably the best man in the world for his job— knew everything—was ready for anything— could manage everyone—and what a Iriend! It's irreparable. Suiely of all men worth saving he ought to have been saved. Yes, saved by force, for only in that way could it have been done."

Here, too, it may be mentioned that during his business career Andrews received many acknowledgements of a gratifying description from those whom in various ways he bad served—amongst others from the White Star Company, the Hamburg American Company and, what I daresay he valued as much, from the stewards of the Olympic. Following the announcement of his marriage, a Committee was organised at the Yard for the purpose of showing him in a tangible way the esteem of the Islanders, but for business reasons, or perhaps feeling a delicacy in accepting a compliment without parallel in the history of the Yard, he whilst making it plain how much the kindly thought had moved him, felt constrained to ask the Committee to desist.

One may end this imperfect chapter with two more tributes, themselves without any great literary merit perhaps, yet testifying sincerely, one thinks, to the love which Andrews inspired in everyone.
Long ago, poor Doctor O'Loughlin wrote in collaboration with the Purser of the Oceanic some verses to be sung to the air Tommy Atkins. Doubtless they have been sung at ship's mess on many a voyage, and perhaps have elsewhere been printed. One verse is given here:

> "Neath a gantry high and mighty she had birth.
> And she'd bulk and length and height and mighty beam.
> And the world was only larger in its girth
> And she seemed to be a living moving dream.
> Then she rode so grandly o'er the sea
> That she seemed a beauty decked in bright array.
> And the whistle sounded loudly As she sailed along so proudly,
> That we all cried out 'She must be quite O.K.'

Thomas Andrews Shipbuilder

Oh Tommy Tommy Andrews we are all so proud of you,
And to say we have the finest ship that e'er was built is true.
May your hand ne'er lose its cunning, we don't care how winds may roar
For we know we have a frigate that can sail from shore to shore."

The second tribute is taken from a Lament, written by the Island poet in the ballad form so popular in Ireland, and circulated widely in the Yard:

"A Queen's Island Trojan, he worked, to the last;
Very -proud we all feel of him here in Belfast;
Our working-men knew him as one of the best—

He stuck to his duty, and God gave him rest."

VI.

IT remains, before giving account of the finest action of his life, to consider briefly, by way of rounding his portrait, what we may call Andrews' outside aspect—the side, that is, he might turn to some Committee of Experts sitting in solemn judgment upon him as a possible candidate for political honours.

That side, it may be said at once, is singularly unpretentious; and indeed when we think of his absorption, heart and soul, in what he knew for him was best, who could expect, or wish, it to be otherwise? In Ulster, heaven knows, are publicists galore, and sufficient men too willing to down tools at any outside horn-blow, that we should the less admire one who spoke only once in public, took no open part in politics, and was not even a strong party-man.

He was, however, a member of the Ulster Reform Club. Twice he was pressed to accept the presidency of Unionist Clubs. Frequently he was urged to permit his nomination for election to the City Council.

The Belfast Harbour Board shared the opinion of one of its leading members that "his youthful vigour, his undoubted ability, and his genial personality, would have made him an acquisitior to this important Board." His fellow-directors, in a resolution of condolence, ex¬pressed their feeling that "not only had the Firm lost a valued and promising leader, but the city an upright and capable citizen, who, had he lived, would have taken a still more conspicuous place in the industrial and com¬mercial world." Even in the south, where admiration of Northerners is not commonly fervent, it was admitted by many that in Andrews Ulster had at last found the makings of a leader.

From such straws, blown in so prevailing a wind, we may determine the estimation in which Andrews, as a prospective citizen, stood amongst those who knew him and their own needs the best; and also perhaps may roughly calculate the possibilities of that future which he himself, in stray minutes of leisure, may have anticipated.

But some there will be doubtless whose admiration of Andrews is the finer because he kept the path of his career straight to its course without any deviation to enticing havens.

Such a man, however, the son of such a father, could not fail to have views on the burning topics of his time, and no estimate of him would be complete which gave these no heed.

He was, we are told, an Imperialist, loving peace and consequently in favour of an unchallengeable Navy. He was a firm Unionist, being convinced that Home Rule would spell financial ruin to Ireland, through the partial loss of British credit, and of the security derived from connection with a strong and prosperous partner. At times he was known to express disapproval of the policy adopted by those Irish Unionists who strove to influence British electors by appeals to passion rather than by means of reasoned argument. Also he felt that Ireland would never be happy and prosperous until agitation ceased and promise of security were offered to the investing capitalist.

Though no believer in modern cities, he was of opinion that an effort should be made to expand and stimulate Irish village life, it seeming to him that a country dependent solely on agriculture was like a man fighting the battle of life with one hand. Were, however, an approved system of agriculture, such as that advocated by Sir Horace Plunkett, joined with a considered scheme of town and village industries, he believed that emigration would cease and Ireland find prosperity.

THE "TITANIC" AND THE "OLYMPIC" BUILDING IN THE LARGEST GANTRY IN THE WORLD

To the practical application of Tariff Reform he saw many difficulties, but thought them not insuperable. In view of the needs of a world-wide and growing Empire, "the necessity of preserving British work for British people," and the injury done to home trade by the unfair competition of protected countries, he judged that the duties upon imported necessities should be materially reduced and a counterbalancing tax levied on all articles of foreign manufacture.

He advocated moderate Social reform on lines carefully designed to encourage thrift, temperance and endeavour; and as one prime means towards improving the condition, both moral and physical, of the workers he would have the State, either directly or through local authorities, provide them with decent homes.

To the consideration of Labour problems, particularly those coming within the scope of his own experience, he gave much thought; and when it is considered that his great popularity with all classes held steady through the recent period of industrial unrest, we may judge that his attitude towards Labour, in the mass as in the unit, was no mere personal expression of friendliness. As his real pals he wanted to help the workers, educate and lift them.

Other things being equal, he always favoured the men who used their heads as well as their hands; and if in the management of their own affairs they used their heads, then also, so much the better for all concerned.

He considered that both in the interests of men and masters, it was well for Labour to be oiganized under capable leaders; but honest agreements should, he thought, be binding on both sides and not liable to governmental interference.

Politicians and others should in their public utterances, he felt, endeavour to educate the workers in the principles of economics relative to trade, wages and the relations between capital and labour ; but publicists who, for party or like reasons, strove to foster class hatreds and strifes he would hang by the heels from a gantry.

Where economically possible, the working day should, he thought, be shortened, especially the day of all toiling in arduous and unwholesome conditions. Similarly he was disposed to favour, when economically possible, encouragement of the workers by means of a system of profit sharing.

He would, furthermore, give them every facility for technical education, but such he knew from experience was of little value unless supplemented by thorough practical knowledge gained in the workshop.

These views and opinions, whatever their intrinsic value in the eyes of experts, are at least interesting. Sooner or later, had Andrews lived, he would perhaps have made them the basis of public pronouncements; and then indeed might his abounding energy, applied in new and luring directions, have carried him to heights of citizenship.

VII.

Happily, there is no need in these pages to attempt any minute estimate of the share Andrews had in building the Titanic.

Such a task, were it feasible, would offer difficulties no less testing than those met courageously by half the world's journalists when attempting to describe the wonders of that ill-fated vessel— her length that of a suburban street, her height the equivalent of a seventeen story building, her elevator cars coursing up and down as through a city hotel, her millionaire suites, her luxuries of squash racquet courts, Turkish and electric bath establishments, salt water swimming pools, glass enclosed sun parlours, verandah cafés, and all.

Probably no one man, was solely responsible for the beautiful thing. She was an evolution rather than a creation, triumphant product of numberless experiments, a perfection embodying who knows what endeavour, from this a little, from that a little more, of human brain and hand and imagination. How many ships were built, how many lost; how many men lived, wrought, and died that the Titanic might be?

So much being said, it may however be said further, that to her building Andrews gave as much of himself as did any other man. All his experience of ships, gained in the yards, on voyages, by long study, was in her; all his deep knowledge, too, gathered during twenty years and now applied in a crowning effort with an ardour that never flagged. It was by the Titanic, "her vast shape slowly assuming the beauty and symmetry which are but a memory to-day," that Mr. Childers met Andrews and noted in him those qualities of zest, rigour, power and simplicity, which impressed him deeply. Yet Andrews then was no whit more enthusiastic, we feel sure, than on any other day of the great ship's fashioning,

THE "TITANIC" LEAVING BELFAST

from the time of her conception slowly down through the long process of calculating, planning, designing, building, fitting, until at last she sailed proudly away to the applause of half the world. Whatever share others had in her, his at least cannot be gainsaid.

As Lord Pirrie's Assistant he had done his part by way of shaping into tangible form the projects of her owners. As Chief Designer and Naval Architect he planned her complete. As Managing Director he saw her grow up, frame by frame, plate by plate, day after day throughout more than two years; watched her grow as a father watches his child grow, assiduously, minutely, and with much the same feelings of parental pride and affection. For Andrews this was his ship, whatever his hand in her: and in that she was "efficiently designed and constructed" as is now established* his fame as a Shipbuilder may well rest. As surely none other did, he knew her inside and out, her every turn and art, the power and beauty of her, from keel to truck— knew her to the last rivet. And because he knew the great ship so well, as a father knows the child born to him, therefore to lose her was heart-break.

On Tuesday morning, April 2nd, 1912, at 6 a.m., the Titanic left Belfast, in ideal weather, and was towed down Channel to complete her trials. On board was Andrews, representing the Firm. Her compasses being adjusted, the ship steamed towards the Isle of Man, and after a satisfactory run returned to the Lough about 6 p.m.

Throughout the whole day Andrews was busy, receiving representatives of the owners, inspecting and superintending the work of internal completion, and taking notes. "Just a line," he wrote to Mrs. Andrews, "to let you know that we got away this morning in

*Report of Mersey Commission, pp. 61 and 71

fine style and have had a very satisfactory trial. We are getting more ship-shape every hour, but there is still a great deal to be done."

Having received letters and transferred workmen, the ship left immediately for Southampton, Andrews still on board and with him, amongst others, the eight brave men from the Island Yard who perished with him. They were :

William Henry Marsh Parr, Assistant Manager Electrical Department.
Roderick Chisholm, Ships' Draughtsman.
Anthony W. Frost, Outside Foreman Engineer.
Robert Knight, Leading Hand Engineer.
William Campbell, Joiner Apprentice.
Alfred Fleming Cunningham, Fitter Apprentice.
Frank Parkes, Plumber Apprentice.
Ennis Hastings Watson, Electrician Apprentice.

During the whole of Wednesday, the 3rd, until midnight, when the ship arrived at Southampton, Andrews was ceaselessly employed going round with representatives of the owners and of the Firm, in taking notes and preparing reports of work still to be done. All the next day, from an early hour, he spent with managers and foremen putting work in hand.

In the evening he wrote to Mrs Andrews: "I wired you this morning of our safe arrival after a very satisfactory trip. The weather was good and everyone most pleasant. I think the ship w'ill clean up all right before sailing on Wednesday": and then he mentions that the doctors refused to allow Lord Pirrie to make the maiden voyage.

Thereafter from day to day, until the date of sailing, he was always busy, taking the owners round ship, interviewing engineers, officials, agents, managers, sub-contractors, discussing with principals the plans of new ships, and superintending generally the work of completion

"Through the various days that the vessel lay at Southampton," writes his Secretary, Mr. Thompson Hamilton, "Mr. Andrews was never for a moment idle. He generally left his hotel about 8.30 for the offices, where he dealt with his correspondence, then went on board until 6.30, when he would return to the offices to sign letters. During the day I took to the ship any urgent papers and he always dealt with them no matter what his business." Nothing he allowed to interfere with duty. He was conscientious to the minutest detail. "He would himself put in their place such things as racks, tables, chairs, berth ladders, electric fans, saying that except he saw everything right he could not be satisfied."

One of the last letters he wrote records serious trouble with the restaurant galley hot press, and directs attention to a design for reducing the number of screws in stateroom hat hooks.

Another of earlier date, in the midst of technicalities about cofferdams and submerged cylinders on the propeller boss, expresses agreement with the owner that the colouring of the pebble dashing on the private promenade decks was too dark, and notes a plan for staining green the wicker furniture on one side of the vessel.

Withal, his thought for others never failed. Now he is arranging for a party to view the ship; now writing to a colleague, "I have always in mind a week's holiday due to you from last summer and shall be glad if you will make arrangements to take these on my return, as, although you may not desire to have them, I feel sure that a week's rest will do you good." On the evening of Sunday, the 7th, he wrote to Mrs. Andrews giving her news of his movements and dwelling upon the plans he had in mind for the future.

On the 9th he wrote: "The Titanic is now about complete and will I think do the old Firm credit to-morrow when we sail."

On the 10th he was aboard at 6 o'clock, and thence until the hour of sailing he spent in a long final inspection of the ship. She pleased him. The old Firm was sure of its credit.

Just before the moorings were cast off he bade goodbye to Mr. Hamilton and the other officials. He seemed in excellent health and spirits. His last words were, "Remember now and keep Mrs. Andrews informed of any news of the vessel."

The Titanic, carrying 2,201 souls, left Southampton punctually at noon on April 10th. There was no departure ceremony. On her way from dock she passed the Majestic and the Philadelphia, both giants of twenty years ago and now by contrast with Leviathan humbled to the stature of dwarfs.

About a mile down the water she passed Test Quay, where the Oceanic and the New York lay berthed. Her wash caused the New York to break her moorings and drift into the Channel. As the Titanic was going dead slow danger of a collision was soon averted," but,"as Andrews wrote that evening, "the situation was decidedly unpleasant."

From Cherbourg he wrote again to Mrs. Andrews: "We reached here in nice time and took on board quite a number of passengers. The two little tenders looked well, you will remember we built them about a year ago. We expect to arrive at Queenstown about 10.30 a.m. tomorrow. The weather is fine and everything shaping for a good voyage. I have a seat at the Doctor's table."

One more letter was received from him by Mrs. Andrews, and only one, this time from Queenstown, and dated April 11th. Everything on board was going splendidly, he said, and he expressed his satisfaction at receiving so much kindness from everyone.

Here all direct testimony ceases. Proudly, in eye of the world, the Titanic sailed Westward from the Irish coast; then for a while disappeared; only to reappear in a brief scene of woefullest tragedy round which the world stayed mute. If, as is almost certain, a chronicle of the voyage was made by Andrews, both it and the family letters he wrote now are gone with him.

But fortunately, we have other evidence, plentiful and well-attested, and on such our story henceforward runs.

The steward, Henry E. Etches, who attended him says, that during the voyage, right to the moment of disaster, Andrews was constantly busy. With his workmen he went about the boat all day long, putting things right and making note of every suggestion of an imper¬fection.

Afterwards in his stateroom, which is described as being full of charts, he would sit for hours, making calculations and drawings for future use.

Others speak of his great popularity with both passengers and crew. "I was proud of him," writes the brave stewardess, Miss May Sloan, of Belfast, whose testimony is so invaluable. "He came from home and he made you feel on the ship that all was right." And then she adds how because of his big, gentle, kindly nature everyone loved him. "It was good to hear his laugh and have him near you. If anything went wrong it was always to Mr. Andrews one went.

Even when a fan stuck in a stateroom, one would say, 'Wait for Mr. Andrews, he'll soon see to it,' and you would find him settling even the little quarrels that arose between ourselves. Nothing came amiss to him, nothing at all. And he was always the same, a nod and a smile or a hearty word whenever he saw you and no matter what he was at."

Two of his table companions, Mr. and Mrs. Albert A. Dick, of Calgary, Alberta, also tell how much they came to love Andrews because of his character, and how good it was to see his pride in the ship, "but upon every occasion, and especially at dinner on Sunday evening, he talked almost constantly about his wife, little girl, mother and family, as well as of his home."

This pre-occupation with home and all there, was noticed too by Miss Sloan. Sometimes, between laughs, he would suddenly fall grave and glance, you might say, back over a shoulder towards Dunallan and Ardara far off near Strangford Lough.

"I was talking to him on the Friday night as he was going into dinner," writes Miss Sloan, in a letter dated from the Lapland on April 27th. "The dear old Doctor* was waiting for him on the stair-landing, and calling him by his Christian name, Tommy. Mr. Andrews seemed loth to go, he wanted to talk about home; he was telling me his father was ill and Mrs. Andrews not so well. I was congratulating him on the beauty and perfection of the ship ; he said the part he did not like was that the

---

* Dr. W. F. N. O'Loughlin, Senior Surgeon of the White Star Line, a close friend of Andrews and his companion on many voyages. Some lines which he helped to write have been quoted. Soon after the ship struck he said to Miss Sloan—" child, things are very bad," and went to his death bravely. His Assistant, Dr. T. E. Simpson, son of an eminent Belfast physician, and himself a physician of much promise, died with him.

Titanic was taking us further away from home every hour. I looked at him and his face struck me as having a very sad expression."

One other glimpse we have of him, then in that brief time of triumph, whilst yet the good ship of his which everyone praised was speeding

Westwards, "in perfectly clear and fine weather," towards the place where "was no moon, the stars were out, and there was not a cloud in the sky." ✳

For more than a week he had been working at such pressure, that by the Friday evening many saw how tired as well as sad he looked: but by the Sunday evening, when his ship was as perfect, so he said, as brains could make her, he was himself again. "I saw him go in to dinner," said Miss Sloan, "he was in good spirits, and I thought he looked splendid."

An hour or two afterwards he went aft to thank the baker for some special bread he had made for him ; then back to his stateroom, where apparently he changed into working clothes, and sat down to write.

He was still writing, it would seem, when the Captain called him.

✳ Report of Mersey Commission, p. 29,

VIII.

On the night of Sunday, 14th April, at 11 40 ship's time, in clear fine weather, near Latitude 41° 46' N., Longitude 50° 14' W., the Titanic collided with the submerged spur of an iceberg and ripped her starboard side ten feet above the level of the keel for a length of about three hundred feet, thereby giving access to the sea in six of her forward compartments. The calamity came with dreadful swiftness. In the vivid words of a stoker, on duty at the time of collision some two hundred and fifty feet from the stem: "All of a sudden the starboard side of the ship came in upon us; it burst like a big gun going off; the water came pouring in and swilled our legs."

Within ten minutes the water rose fourteen feet above the keel in five of the compartments; afterwards it rose steadily in all six; and by midnight had submerged the lower deck in the foremost hold. Yet so gentle apparently was the shock of contact that among the passengers, and probably among most of the crew as well, it was only the stopping of the engines that warned them of some happening; whilst for a considerable time, so quietly the great ship lay on the flat sea, such confidence had all in her strength, and so orderly was everything, that to many, almost to the last, it seemed impossible that disaster had come.*

"At first we did not realise," says Mr. Albert Dick,†" that the Titanic was mortally wounded. . . . I do not believe that anyone on her realised she was going to sink."

---

* Mersey Commission Report,; Sir William White's letter to the Times, dated May 14th.
† New York Herald, April 20th, 1912

Mr. Dick goes on to record that, in his view, nothing deserved more praise than the conduct of Andrews after the ship had struck. "He was on hand at once and said that he was going below to investigate. We begged him not to 'go, but he insisted, saying he knew the ship as no one else did and that he might be able to allay the fears of the passengers. He went.

"As the minutes flew by we did not know what to do or which way to turn. . . . Captain Smith was everywhere doing his best to calm the rising tide of fear. . . But in the minds of most of us there was . . . the feeling that something was going to happen, and we waited for Mr. Andrews to come back.

"When he came we hung upon his words, and they were these : 'There is no cause for any excitement. All of you get what you can in the way of clothes and come on deck as soon as you can. She is torn to bits below, but she will not sink if her after bulkheads hold.'

"It seemed almost impossible that this could be true . . . and many in the crowd smiled, thinking this was merely a little extra knowledge that Mr. Andrews saw fit to impart. . . ."

It is almost certain that Andrews, who knew the ship as no one else did, realised at his first sight of her wounds—a three hundred feet gash, six compartments open to the sea and perhaps twenty feet of water in one or more of them— that she was doomed. Possibly with some of his faithful assistants, probably with Captain Smith, he had made a thorough examination of the damaged side, reporting to the Captain as result of his examination that the ship could not live more than an hour and a half, and advising him to clear away the boats.

How this order was carried out, with what skill and unselfishness on the part of Captain Smith and his officers, has been told elsewhere* in full detail; nor is it necessary to record further here than that eventually, after two

hours of heroic work, a total of 652 lives left the Titanic in eighteen boats. Subsequently 60 more were rescued from the sea, or transferred from the collapsibles, making a sum total of 712 rescued by the Carpathia. 712 out of 2,201: it seems tragically few! Yet at midnight it may have seemed to Andrews that fewer still could be saved, for not even he hoped that his ship could live for two hours and twenty minutes more.

As he came up from the grim work of investigation he saw Miss Sloan and told her that as an accident had happened it would be well, just by way of precaution, to get her passengers to put on warm clothing and their life belts and assemble on the Boat deck. But she read his face, "which had a look as though he were heart broken,". and asked him if the accident were not serious. He said it was very serious ; then, bidding her keep the bad news quiet for fear of panic, he hurried away to the work of warning and rescue.

Another stewardess gives an account of Andrews, bareheaded and insufficiently clad against the icy cold, going quietly about bidding the attendants to rouse all passengers and get them up to the boats.

Overhearing him say to Captain Smith on the Upper deck, "Well, three have gone already, Captain," she ran to the lower stairway and to her surprise found water within six steps of her feet. Whereupon she hurried above to summon help, and returning met Andrews, who told her to advise passengers to leave the Upper deck.

*E.g., Mersey Commission Report, pp. 39-41

Ten minutes went. The water had crept further up the stairway. Again Andrews came to her and said, "Tell them to put on warm clothing, see that everyone has a lifebelt and get them all up to the Boat deck."

Another fifteen minutes went. The top of the stairway was now nearly awash. A second time Andrews came. " Open up all the spare rooms," he ordered. "Take out all lifebelts and spare blankets and distribute them." This was done. Attendants and passengers went above to the Boat deck. But returning for more belts, the stewardess again met Andrews. He asked her whether all the ladies had left their rooms. She answered " Yes, but would make sure."

"Go round again," said he ; and then, "Did I not tell you to put on your life-belt. Surely you have one?"

She answered "Yes, but I thought it mean to wear it."
"Never mind that," said he. "Now, if you value your life, put on your coat and belt, then walk round the deck and let the passengers see you." "He left me then," writes the stewardess, "and that was the last I saw of what I consider a true hero and one of whom his country has cause to be proud."

In how far Andrews' efforts and example were the means of averting what might well have been an awful panic, cannot be said ; but sure it is that all one man could do in such service, both personally and by way of assisting the ship's officers, was done by him. "He was here, there and everywhere," says Miss Sloan, "looking after everybody, telling the women to put on lifebelts, telling the stewardesses to hurry the women up to the boats, all about everywhere, thinking of everyone but himself." Others tell a similar story, how calm and unselfish he was, now pausing on his way to the engine-room to reassure some passengers, now earnestly begging women to be quick, now helping one to put on her lifebelt—" all about everywhere, thinking of everybody but himself."

It is certain also that on the Boat deck he gave invaluable help to the officers and men engaged in the work of rescue. Being familiar with the boats' tackle and arrangement he was able to aid effectively at their launching; and it was whilst going quietly from boat to boat, probably in those tragic intervals during which the stewardess watched the water creep up the stairway, that he was heard to say: "Now, men, remember you are Englishmen. Women and children first."

Some twenty minutes before the end, when the last distress signal had been fired in vain, when all that Upper deck and the Fore deck as well were ravaged by the sea, there was a crush and a little confusion near the place where the few remaining boats were being lowered, women and children shrinking back, some afraid to venture, some preferring to stay with their husbands, a few perhaps in the grip of cold and terror.

Then Andrews came and waving his arms gave loud command: "Ladies, you must get in at once. There is not a minute to lose. You cannot pick and choose your boat. Don't hesitate. Get in, get in!"

They obeyed him. Do they remember to-day, any of them, that to him they, as so many more, may owe their lives?

A little way back from that scene, Miss Sloan stood calmly waiting and seeing Andrews for the last time. She herself was not very anxious to leave the ship, for all her friends were staying behind and she felt it was mean to go. But the command of the man, who for nearly two hours she had seen doing as splendidly as now he was doing, came imperatively. " Don't hesitate! There's not a moment to lose. Get in!" So she stepped into the last boat and was saved.

It was then five minutes past two. The Titanic had fifteen minutes more to live.

Well, all was done now that could be done, and the time remaining was short. The Forecastle head was under water. All around, out on the sea, so calm under those wonderful stars, the boats were scattered, some near, some a mile away or more, the eyes of most in them turned back upon the doomed ship as one by one her port lights, that still burnt row above row in dreadful sloping lines, sank slowly into darkness. Soon the lines would tilt upright, then flash out and flash bright again; then, as the engines crashed down through the bulkheads, go out once more, and leave that awful form standing up against the sky, motionless, black, preparing for the final plunge.

But that time was not yet. Some fifteen minutes were left: and in those mintues we still have sight of Andrews.

One met him, bareheaded and carrying a lifebelt, on his way to the bridge perhaps to bid the Captain goodbye.

Later, an assistant steward saw him standing alone in the smoking-room, his arms folded over his breast and the belt lying on a table near him. The steward asked him, "Aren't you going to have a try for it, Mr. Andrews?" He never answered or moved, "just stood like one stunned."
What did he see as he stood there, alone, rapt? We who know the man and his record can believe that before him was home and all the loved ones there, wife and child, father and mother, brothers and sister, relatives, friends— that picture and all it meant to him then and there; and besides, just for a moment maybe, and as background to all that, swift realisation of the awful tragedy ending his life, ending his ship.

But whatever he saw, in that quiet lonely minute, it did not hold or unman him. Work— work—he must work to the bitter end.

Some saw him for the last time, down in the Engineroom, with Chief engineer Bell and Archie Frost and the other heroes, all toiling like men to keep the lights going and the pumps at work.

Others saw him, a few minutes before the end, on the Boat deck, our final and grandest sight of him, throwing deck chairs overboard to the unfortunates struggling in the water below.

Then, with a slow long slanting dive, the Titanic went down, giving to the sea her short- spanned life and with it the life of Thomas Andrews. So died this noble man. We may hope that he lies, as indeed he might be proud to lie, in the great ship he had helped to fashion.

APPENDIX

APPENDIX

AT the request of the Family the publishers have inserted the following cables and letters which were received when the news of the disaster first became public.

Cable dated New York, 19th April, 1912, addressed to Mr. James Moore, Belfast.

Interview Titanic's officers. All unanimous Andrews heroic unto death, thinking only safety others. Extend heartfelt sympathy to all.

JAMES MONTGOMERY.

Cable dated 21st April, 1912, received by the White Star Line in Liverpool from their Office in New York.

After accident Andrews ascertained damage, advised passengers to put on heavy clothing and prepare to leave vessel. Many were sceptical about the serious-ness of the damage, but impressed by Andrews' knowledge and personality, followed his advice, and so saved their lives. He assisted many women and children to lifeboats. When last seen, officers say, he was throwing overboard deck chairs and other objects to people in the water, his chief concern the safety of everyone but himself.

Extract from letter written by Lord Pirrie to his sister, Mrs. Thomas Andrews, Sen.

"A finer fellow than Tommie never lived, and by his death—unselfishly beautiful to the last—we are bereft of the strong young life upon which such reliance had come to be placed by us elders who loved and needed him."

Thomas Andrews Shipbuilder

Copy of Letter received by Mrs. „Thomas Andrews, Jun.. from Mr. Bruce Ismay.

30 JAMES STREET,
Liverpool, 31 st May, 1912.

DEAR MRS. ANDREWS,

Forgive me for intruding upon your grief, but I feel I must send you a line to convey my most deep and sincere sympathy with you in the terrible loss you have suffered. It is impossible for me to express in words all I feel, or make you realise how truly sorry I am for you, or how my heart goes out to you. I knew your husband for many years, and had the highest regard for him, and looked upon him as a true friend. No one who had the pleasure of knowing him could fail to realise and appreciate his numerous good qualities and he will be sadly missed in his profession. Nobody did more for the White Star Line, or was more loyal to its interests than your good husband, and I always placed the utmost reliance on his judgment.

If we miss him and feel his loss so keenly, what your feelings must be I cannot think. Words at such a time are useless, but I could not help writing to you to tell you how truly deeply I feel for you in your grief and sorrow.

Yours sincerely,
BRUCE ISMAY.

Letter from Sir Horace Plunkett to Right Hon. Thomas Andrews.

THE PLUNKETT HOUSE,
Dublin, 19th April, 1912.

MY DEAR ANDREWS,

No act of friendship is so difficult as the letter of condolence upon the loss of one who is near and dear. Strive as we may to avoid vapid conventionality, we find ourselves drifting into reflections upon the course of nature, the cessation of suffering, the worse that might have been, and such offers of comfort to others which we are conscious would be of little help to ourselves. In writing to you and your wife on the sorrow of two worlds, which has fallen so heavily upon your home and family, I feel no such difficulty. There is no temptation to be conventional, but it is hard to express in words the very real consolation which will long be cherished by the wide circle of those now bitterly deploring the early death of one who was clearly marked out for a great career in the chief doing part of Irish life.

Of the worth of your son I need not speak to you— nothing I could say of his character or capacity could add to your pride in him. But you ought to know that we all feel how entirely to his own merits was due the extraordinary rapidity of his rise and the acknowledged certainty of his leadership in what Ulster stands for before the world.

When I first saw him in the shipyard he was in a humble position, enjoying no advantage on account of your relationship to one of his employers. Even then, as on many subsequent occasions, I learned, or heard from my Irish fellow- workers, that this splendid son of yours had the best kind of public spirit—that which made you and Sinclair save the Recess Committee at its crisis

It may be that the story of your poor boy's death will never be told, but I seem to see it all. I have just come off the sister ship, whose captain was a personal friend, as was the old doctor who went with him to the Titanic. I have been often in the fog among the icebergs.

I have heard, in over sixty voyages, many of those awful tales of the sea. I know enough to be aware that your son might easily have saved himself on grounds of public duty none could gainsay. What better witness could be found to tell the millions who would want and had a right to know why the great ship failed, and how her successors could be made, as she was believed to be, unsinkable? None of his breed could listen to such promptings of the lower self when the call came to show to what height the real man in him could rise.

I think of him displaying the very highest quality of courage—the true heroism—with-out any of the stimulants which the glamour and prizes of battle supply—doing all he could for the women and children—and then going grimly and silently to his glorious grave.

So there is a bright side to the picture which you of his blood and his widow must try to share with his and your friends—with the thousands who will treasure his memory. It will help you in your bereavement, and that is why I intrude upon your sorrow with a longer letter than would suffice to tender to you and Mrs. Andrews and to all your family circle a tribute of heartfelt sympathy.

Pray accept this as coming not only from myself but also from those intimately associated with me in the Irish work which brought me, among other blessings, the friendship of men like yourself.

>Believe me,
>Yours always,
>HORACE PLUNKETT.

Thomas Andrews Shipbuilder

Thomas Andrews Shipbuilder

Made in the USA
Monee, IL
27 February 2023